Primary
Source
Pro

Research

Primary Source
Documents

Diaries, Letters, Journals, and More!

by Kelly Boswell

a capstone imprint

First Facts are published by Pebble
1710 Roe Crest Drive, North Mankato, Minnesota 56003
www.mycapstone.com

Library of Congress Cataloging-in-Publication Data
Library of Congress Cataloging-in-Publication-Data is on file with the Library of Congress.
ISBN 978-1-9771-0281-2 (library binding)
ISBN 978-1-9771-0511-0 (paperback)
ISBN 978-1-9771-0291-1 (ebook pdf)

Editorial Credits
Erika L. Shores, editor; Charmaine Whitman, designer; Jo Miller, media researcher;
Laura Manthe, production specialist

Image Credits
Capstone Studio: Karon Dubke, 19 (both); Alamy: John Frost Newspapers, 11; Getty Images:
Fotosearch/Stringer, 7; Library of Congress, 21; National Archives and Records Administration,
Cover (top left), 9, 13, 15 (both); Shutterstock: David Smart, Cover (top right), Everett Historical, 8,
Lane V. Erickson, 5 (top), Maria Dryfhout, 5 (bottom), sonofpromise, Cover (bottom left),
wavebreakmedia, Cover (bottom right); Wikimedia: Library of Congress, 17

Design Elements
Shutterstock: zao4nik

Printed and bound in the United States of America.
PA49

Table of Contents

What Is a Primary Source Document?

When you were born, a piece of paper was filled out about you. The paper is called a birth certificate. In school, your teacher fills out a report card on you. Both are **primary source** documents. These important papers tell us about people, places, and events.

primary source—an original, first-hand account of an event or time period

birth certificate

STATE OF
DEPARTMENT OF HEALTH AND W...
BUREAU OF HEALTH POLICY AND VITAL STATI...

CERTIFICATE OF LIVE BIRTH

State File No. 11...

COUNTY OF BI...

report card

Studies, etc.	1st mo.	2d mo.	3d mo.	4th mo.	5th mo.	6th mo.	7th mo.	8th mo.	9th mo.	10th mo.	Average
Reading	B	B	B+	B+	B+	B+	B+	B+	B		
Spelling	C	B-	B+	B	97	A-	B+	A-	B+		
Writing	A-	A-	A-	A-	A	A-	A-	A-	A-		
Drawing											
Arithmetic	C+	B-	B+	C	C+	C	C+	B	B+		
Grammar	B	B	B	C	C+	B-	C+	B	B		
Geography	—	—	B	B+	B+	B	B	B+	B		
History											

5

Different Kinds of Primary Source Documents

A primary source document is a written record. A diary is one primary source document. Others are newspapers, letters, and written laws. Every piece of paper left behind by people is full of clues. They tell us about everyday life or **historical** events.

Fact

In the 1850s African Americans in the southern United States were enslaved. Charlotte Forten grew up in the North where slavery was not allowed. Her diary shows us her thoughts at that time.

historical—to do with people or events of the past

Saturday, May 27, 1854

Returned home, read the Anti-Slavery [news] papers, and then went down to the [train] to meet father; he had arrived in Boston early in the morning, regretted very much that he had not reached there in the evening before to attend the great meeting at Faneuil Hall. He says that the excitement in Boston is very great; the trial of the poor man [Anthony Burns] takes place on Monday. We scarcely dare to think what may be the result. . . .

Anthony Burns had escaped slavery but was later captured in Boston.

Charlotte Forten

Before phones, people used **telegrams** to send information quickly. Telegrams are primary sources.

To study primary source documents, first read the entire document carefully. Notice any dates or names. Look to see if any words catch your attention.

Fact

A telegram was sent to the people in charge at Pearl Harbor. Sadly the message arrived too late. The attack had already begun.

telegram—a written message sent over a long distance; a machine called a telegraph used electrical signals to send the message by wire or radio

A telegram sent to other U.S. Navy bases tells of the Japanese attack on U.S. ships in Pearl Harbor.

The message was sent on December 7, 1941.

BOSTON NAVY YARD 7 9 41

FIRST NAVAL DISTRICT — RECEIVED DISPATCH — N. A. S. Squantum

FROM: CONFIDENTIAL CALLS

RELAYED TO:

TO:

INFO:

			DATE	TIME
PRIORITY	RESTRICTED	RELEASED BY	7 DEC 41	
ROUTINE	CONFIDENTIAL		REF. NR.	
DEFERRED	SECRET	SENT BY		

HEADING: NZW V NCO NR1 / NSS F NR977 Z ØF2 183Ø ØF3 ØF4 1FØ Ø BT

AIR RAID ON PEARL HARBOR X THIS IS NOT DRILL

The message is short, yet powerful!

TOR 2ØØ4/AD/NCO NR 1/3195 KC/7 DEC 41

ACTION OFFICER .... O. O. D.

The telegram says Pearl Harbor was attacked from the air, also known as an air raid.

The air raid was real.

9

When **examining** primary source documents, imagine that you're using a magnifying glass to look closely at the document. Notice the pictures, captions, and the big, bold words. Then, carefully read all of the words.

"Children love television, and with the advanced Magnascope system they can watch the screen for hours without straining precious eyes."

Children still love TV today. But we know it's not a great idea for kids to "watch the screen for hours!"

A radio-phonograph was a machine that played radio stations and records. That's how people listened to music in 1949!

This picture shows us that TVs looked very different in 1949 than they look today.

examine—to inspect or look at something carefully

This ad appeared in a magazine in 1949.

America's Great Value *

AMERICAN TRADITIONAL *Radio-Phonograph. Provision is made for TV installation at any time—in upper section now used for record storage. Record albums extra.* **$298.50**

Complete combination with Magnascope Television (full-size 12¼-in. picture tube). Record albums extra. **$645.00**

People dressed differently in 1949.

Modern Magic by Magnavox
...within reach of every family

YOU can give your children wonders Aladdin never knew. The twentieth century magic of Magnavox, America's finest television receiver and radio-phonograph, is for everyone!

Although you might gladly give more for the greater value Magnavox quality assures, you can have a magnificent Magnavox Radio-Phonograph in your home for as little as $298.50—for $299.50, a television receiver. Magnavox is *all* America's great television-radio-phonograph value.

REGENCY *AM-FM-Short wave Radio-Phonograph (4 speakers).*

Children love television, and with the advanced Magnascope system they can watch the screen for hours without straining precious eyes. Magnavox produces big, steady pictures unmatched for sharpness, clarity and contrast.

4 Hours Continuous Music. Magnavox plays long-playing and conventional records automatically! Provision is made for playing others manually.

See your Magnavox Dealer for a demonstration. The Magnavox Company, Ft. Wayne 4, Indiana.
Prices subject to change without notice.

METROPOLITAN *Television Receiver with 10-in. picture tube.*

$595.00

$299.50
TABLE EXTRA

the magnificent
Magnavox
radio phonograph + television

✳ **No obsolescence with Magnavox!** Provision is made so that Magnavox owners will be able to receive *all* proposed UHF channels when and if they are established in addition to *all* present VHF channels.

11

Be a History Explorer!

One way you can gather clues from primary source documents is by asking and answering the "Five W Questions:"

Who?	Who wrote the document? To whom is it written?
What?	What is the document about?
Where?	Where did the events in the document happen?
When?	When was the document written?
Why?	Why was it written? What was the author's purpose?

What:
Pam is writing to ask President Nixon to stop the war in the country of Vietnam.

Why:
Pam wants the president to end the war in Vietnam. She hopes the people in the United States will calm down.

Where:
The letter doesn't tell us where Pam Kaplan lived.

December 7, 1970

Dear President Nixon,
    Please stop the war
in VietNam my cousin is in.
    And I want the United
States to settle down.
                Sincerely yours,
                Pam Kaplan

Who:
This letter was written by Pam Kaplan. It is written to President Richard Nixon.

Reading documents like this may lead us to ask more questions:

- *What was the war in Vietnam about?*

- *What did Pam mean when she talked about wanting the United States to settle down?*

Your turn!

Use the "Five W Questions" to study the response to Pam's letter.

Who?	Who wrote the document? To whom is it written?
What?	What is the document about?
Where?	Where did the events in the document happen?
When?	When was the document written?
Why?	Why was it written? What was the author's purpose?

January 15, 1971

Dear Pam:

On behalf of the President, I wish to acknowledge your letter and to thank you for your comments. He wants you to know that he and his advisers are doing everything they can to obtain peace in Vietnam and to solve our problems at home.

With the President's best wishes, and his gratitude for your cousin's service to our country,

Sincerely,

Noble M. Melencamp
Staff Assistant
to the President

President Richard Nixon

Miss Pam Kaplan
3257 Cedarbrook Road
Cleveland Heights, Ohio 44118

JEW:pb

- *What questions do you have after reading this letter?*

Billboards can be primary sources. It's hard to know who writes the words for billboards. But we can guess this writer wanted people to vote against Woodrow Wilson. Some words are printed larger and some words smaller. People often use larger letters for the most important words.

Fact

In the early 1900s, women could not vote or hold public office. In 1920 the 19th **Amendment** became law. Women could vote in all U.S. states.

amendment—a statement that is added to a document

This billboard from 1916 tells women in Colorado to vote for a president who will support woman **suffrage**.

suffrage—the right to vote in political elections

Different Views, Different Ideas

You and your friend are playing at the park. From the top of the slide the park looks one way. Your friend on the ground sees the park in another way. You and your friend have different **perspectives** on the same park.

Events from the past can look different to different people. When we look at things from more than one perspective, it helps us learn more.

perspective—a particular way of looking at something or considering something

view from top of slide

view from bottom of slide

19

Primary source documents often only show us one perspective. We need to study them along with other kinds of primary sources.

Visuals, like this cartoon, can help us see history from someone else's point of view.

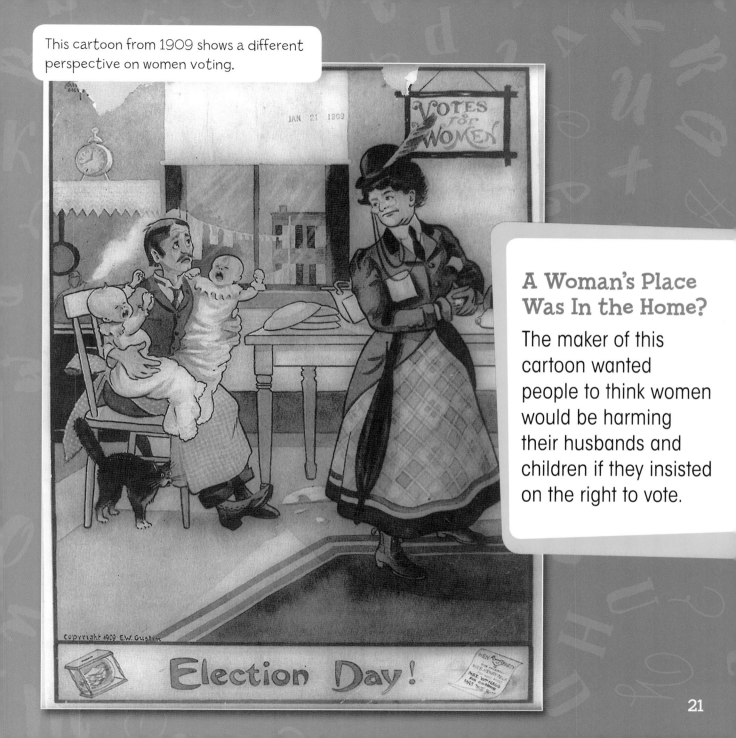

This cartoon from 1909 shows a different perspective on women voting.

A Woman's Place Was In the Home?

The maker of this cartoon wanted people to think women would be harming their husbands and children if they insisted on the right to vote.

Glossary

amendment—a statement that is added to a document

document—a written or printed paper that contains information or evidence

examine—to inspect or look at something carefully

historical—to do with people or events of the past

perspective—a particular way of looking at something or considering something

primary source—an original, first-hand account of an event or time period

suffrage—the right to vote in political elections

telegram—a written message sent over a long distance; a machine called a telegraph used electrical signals to send the message by wire or radio

Read More

Burns, Kylie. *Be a Diary Detective.* Be a Document Detective. New York: Crabtree Publishing Company, 2017.

Clapper, Nikki Bruno. *Learning About Primary Sources.* Media Literacy for Kids. North Mankato, Minn.: Capstone Press, 2016.

Internet Sites

Use FactHound to find Internet sites related to this book.

Visit *www.facthound.com*

Just type in 9781977102812 and go.

Check out projects, games and lots more at **www.capstonekids.com**

Critical Thinking Questions

1. A document is anything that has been printed or written down to communicate, record, or prove something. Give an example of a document that you have seen recently at home or at school. What kind of information was included in this document?

2. Why is it important to think about other perspectives when looking at primary source documents? Use details from the text to support your answer.

3. How would looking at a photograph *and* a document from the same time period help you learn more?

Index